Things to do in
Pre-school
Children's Worship

BOOK TWO

Susan Sayers

Kevin
Mayhew

First published in 2000 by
KEVIN MAYHEW LTD
Buxhall
Stowmarket
Suffolk IP14 3BW

Things To Do in Pre-school Children's Worship, Book Two is adapted from
Living Stones, Year B, by Susan Sayers, published by Kevin Mayhew Ltd, 1999

0 1 2 3 4 5 6 7 8 9

ISBN 1 84003 535 8
Catalogue No 1500348

Cover design by Jonathan Stroulger
Edited by Peter Dainty
Typesetting by Louise Selfe

Printed in Great Britain

Foreword

Working with pre-school children is both a challenge and a privilege. The way young children are met and welcomed, talked and listened to, when they first encounter children's ministry, will have a profound effect on their spiritual growth. It is through the good humour, care and friendliness of those they meet that they will begin to realise how much God loves them.

In all your planning, keep aware of how it will seem from the children's point of view. Is the area attractive and inviting? Is the atmosphere orderly and therefore unthreatening? Are people talking at a speed they can cope with, and giving them time to reply without pressure? Do people genuinely seem to like them and want them to be happy? Is considerate love and fairness expressed in actions as well as in the teaching? Is it fun?

These things are so important because the children will be learning more from the way things are done and from the people they interact with than from the teaching content, valuable though this obviously is.

This book provides you with ideas of things to do with pre-school children, grouped under thematic headings. Each session includes a Bible verse illustrating the theme for the day, a variety of 'doing and learning' activities, and a prayer. You can select and adapt the ideas to suit your particular group. Vary the media the children work with – crayons, finger paints, sponge painting, printing, collage, chalks and pastels are all fun to use. Pray for the children and their families, and read the Bible verses before you plan, so as to incorporate your own valuable insights.

I hope the ideas in this book will help the children in your churches and schools to grow strong and healthy in their faith.

SUSAN SAYERS

Acknowledgements

Scriptures quoted from the *Good News Bible* published by The Bible Societies/HarperCollins Publishers Ltd, UK. © American Bible Society, 1966, 1971, 1976, 1992.

Over the earth is a mat of green used by permission of Oxford University Press, Great Clarendon Street, Oxford, OX2 6DP.

Contents

THE LORD OUR GOD

Invisible God

Words from the Bible

No one has ever seen God, but if we love one another, God lives in union with us, and his love is made perfect in us.

1 John 4:12

Doing and learning

Go outside and feel the wind. Work out where it's coming from, and watch what it does to such things as a piece of thread, a balloon, our clothes, and blown bubbles.

Come back inside and sit in a circle, talking about the wind. What did it feel like on our skin? What did it do? Was the wind real? Could we see it? No! The wind and air are invisible, but we know they are very real. How? Because we can feel the wind and see what it does.

The wind is very useful because it can teach us about God. Like the wind, God's love and closeness to us can't be seen, but it is very, very real. We can feel that God loves us. We can see all around us the beautiful world God has made. Like the wind, we can see the good things God does.

Praying

I can't see the wind
but I can feel it's there.
I can't see you, Lord God,
but I can feel your love!

Finding God

Words from the Bible

'. . . and if you search for him with all your heart, you will find him.'

Deuteronomy 4:29

Doing and learning

Set up an edible treasure hunt, leading the children from one numbered box to the next. Spread the boxes around the edges of the room. Give them each a length of string, with a twiglet tied to one end. (This stops them losing the other things off the end.) In numerical order they thread on an object from each box. They should each end up with their strings looking identically threaded. Box one contains hula hoops (the edible sort) box two has polos, box three has jelly rings and box four has biscuits with a hole in the middle. Those with the right order on the string can eat their necklace.

Talk about our funny treasure hunt. We had to seek for the right number on the box, and get that right. Then we had to do something with what we found. That led us on to the next thing to seek – we found the treasure as we went along, didn't we? And it was treasure that tasted good.

The Bible tells us that we are to seek God as we live our lives. It's a bit like our treasure hunt. We seek, or search, for God by looking out for his love, just as we looked out for the numbers on the boxes. We might find God's love in helping someone, being friendly, enjoying God's beautiful world or talking over our fears and worries with God. There are lots of different ways we can find God's love around, just as there were lots of different tasty things to thread on our string. Our strings were filled up with all sorts of tasty things, and our lives will be filled up with the love of God as we seek him.

Seeking God will help us to know what is right and good, and that will make us happy as Jesus' friends.

Ask if any of them helped someone to find any of the boxes. Thank them for doing that. God wants us to help others to seek him as well. We could invite them to church, or lend them one of our favourite Bible stories, and we can pray for them. That way we will be helping them to get to know our lovely God.

Praying

As I get to know you, Jesus,
I love you more and more.
You're kind and good,
you're strong and brave,
and I'm glad you are my friend.

Seeing God

Words from the Bible

No one has ever seen God. The only Son, who is the same as God and is at the Father's side, he has made him known.

John 1:18

Praying

Thank you, Jesus,
for showing us
what God is like.

Doing and learning

Cut up a magic painting book and supply clean water and brushes, so the children can watch a coloured picture emerging. Alternatively, draw simple pictures (like a sun or a house) on white paper with a candle and let the children paint a colour wash over them to reveal the pictures.

Talk about how we couldn't at first see the colours or the pictures, but they were there, hidden, waiting for us to find them.

We can't see God, either. That doesn't mean God isn't there; it means he is there hidden from our sight. We can look around us, up into the sky and down into the deep seas, and know God must be very clever and important to make all this.

But the one who most explains to us what God is like is Jesus.

What is Jesus like? He loves people, whoever they are, however poor or rich they are, and however young or old they are. He helps them, makes them better and chats with them. He is a good friend. He never lets anyone down. He forgives people even when they are really nasty to him.

The more we get to know Jesus, the more we will be finding out about what God is like.

God's Glorious Light

Words from the Bible

God is light, and there is no darkness at all in him.   *1 John 1:5*

Doing and learning

Use a set of Christmas tree lights, strung across a notice board or round a door frame. If you haven't access to any fairy lights, bring a couple of bedside lamps and a multisocket, so you can turn them all on and off from one switch. Everyone jumps and dances around the room, but whenever the lights go on they stop and face them, standing completely still.

When everyone is sitting in a circle, turn on the fairy lights, make the room as dark as possible and light some candles, standing them on a mirror or some foil so that the lights are reflected. As you light the candles have some quiet music playing, and talk about how good light is, and how beautiful. Draw the children's attention to the colour of the flames, and the bright reflections. Remind everyone that God is here with us, and he loves us and our families very much. For a short while, encourage everyone to sit here very still in the candlelight with the music playing, in God's company. Then explain how we often think of God as being like light, because he is so full of goodness and loveliness. The prayer can be sung (to the tune of *See-saw, Marjorie Daw*) as you sit around the candles.

Praying

Jesus, Jesus,
Lord of earth and heaven,
Jesus, Jesus,
Lord of earth and heaven!

God Helps Us Understand

Words from the Bible

How wonderful are the things the Lord does! All who are delighted with them want to understand them.   *Psalm 111:2*

Doing and learning

Have a time of sharing news, or let different children share with the others something they have learnt how to do.

Spread all the pieces from a jigsaw puzzle over the floor in the circle, but don't show a picture of the completed puzzle. Talk about how we can put it together. First we can look for pieces with straight edges as they will make the edge of the picture. (Do this in turns.) Point out how much easier it would be if we had a picture to help us.

There are lots of things in life which are a big puzzle to us, and we find them very hard to understand. Perhaps we don't understand how dogs bark, why grown-ups talk so long on the phone, what makes heavy planes stay up in the sky, why Mum was cross with us that time, why Dad wasn't cross with us last week, how some people can be cruel to animals, why some people have asthma, why some people are very rich and others very poor.

Our life is full of puzzles. And we are always trying to work the puzzles out.

God understands all the puzzles, and knows why everything is as it is, and how. It's as if God holds the finished picture. So when we're puzzled about anything at all in life, we can ask God to help us understand. (Produce the jigsaw picture.) Bit by bit, if we keep working with God and with each other (talk as you work together on the puzzle), we'll start to understand some of those puzzles, even before we get to heaven!

Praying

Over the earth is a mat of green
over the green is dew,
over the dew are the arching trees,
over the trees, the blue.
Across the blue are scudding clouds,
over the clouds, the sun,
over it all is the love of God,
blessing us every one.

(Ruth Brown
© Oxford University Press)

God Loves Everyone

Words from the Bible

God is love, and whoever lives in love lives in union with God and God lives in union with him.   *1 John 4:16*

Doing and learning

Have enough small gifts as prizes for each child to have one. Keep these hidden. Put some folded pieces of paper in a hat and tell the children that whoever picks the piece of paper with a smiley face on it will be able to have a prize! Hype this up a bit so they are all really hoping to be the lucky one. Pass round the hat, and tell each child to pick a piece of paper but not to open it until you say. When everyone has their paper, let them all open them up and discover that they have all won a prize. Give out the prizes with love from the church.

Talk about what it feels like to be left out, and how it feels when we are the chosen ones. With our God no one is ever left out and we are all special to him, even though we are all different. God doesn't just love those with long hair in bunches, because God loves everyone! He doesn't just love those who are wearing stripes, because God loves everyone! Or those who eat without making a mess, because God loves everyone! He doesn't just love those who go to our church, or those on television. Why not? Because God loves everyone! He doesn't just love those who are good at football, or those who live with both Mum and Dad. Why not? Because God loves everyone! He doesn't just love nice people. He doesn't just love good people. Do you know why? *Because God loves everyone!*

Praying

Every person I can see
is loved by Jesus, just like me!
Whoever I am, whatever I do,
you love me, Jesus! And that's true.

God Hears Our Prayers

Words from the Bible

I love the Lord, because he hears me; he listens to my prayers. He listens to me every time I call to him.   *Psalm 116:1-2*

Doing and learning

Play the singing game *Here we go round the mulberry bush*, with lots of busy verses, such as 'This is the way we clean the car/carry the shopping/hoover the hall/make the packed lunches'.

Talk together about being busy, and all the things that need to be done each day and each week. Sometimes we have to wait to tell our news or talk over a worry we have because people are too busy to listen straightaway. They might say, 'Just wait till I've got the dinner on', or 'till I've driven round this roundabout', or 'till we've paid at the checkout'.

But God is always ready to listen to us, because he isn't stuck in time like us. He can give us his full attention straightaway, wherever we are. He never rushes us or tells us to wait. He's always ready to listen to our worries and fears, and enjoy our news and jokes with us.

Praying

Thank you, Lord,
for listening when we pray.
You're never too busy
to hear what we say.

GOD'S CREATION

Wonderful Creator

Words from the Bible

God created the heavens and stretched them out; he fashioned the earth and all that lives there; he gave life and breath to all its people.   *Isaiah 42:5*

Doing and learning

Take the children outside to look up at the sky and wonder at the clouds and the stars which are out there but which we can't see because the sun is shining. Draw their attention to the way they are breathing in the air that is all around them, and let them swish their arms around to feel it moving against them.

Back inside, look at our hands and the skin on them which keeps our insides together, protects us so well and exactly fits us! All the things we have been looking at are the work of someone so amazing that our eyes can't even see him – we can only see the wonderful things he has made.

And his name is God. We are only alive here because God invented us. God invented the universe we live in. God sees everything that goes on. He is watching us now. He is listening to us now – not just to what we're saying, but to what we are all thinking as well! He hears us feeling sad when we're sad, grumpy when we're grumpy, and happy when we're happy. He knows when we try hard to be kind, even when we don't really want to. He knows when we feel sorry for someone and want to help them. He knows when we are being silly or unkind.

God knows each of us and every other person really well, even if we don't know that much about him yet. But as we get to know God more, we'll find out that he is completely good and completely loving as well as completely powerful.

Praying

Star maker, sky maker,
help me to see
that God who made everything
knows and loves ME!

God's Beautiful World (1)

Words from the Bible

From the sky you send rain on the hills, and the earth is filled with your blessings.   *Psalm 104:13*

Doing and learning

Share some ordinary things and look at them carefully. For example, bring a rosehip, break it open and look at all the seeds inside, a peapod with its neatly arranged peas, a selection of bright colours in feathers, flowers, stones and shells. Provide some tubes for the children to look down, so they can focus on the objects. They can also look through a magnifying glass at various things. Look up at the huge sky and the clouds, or the rain or shadows. Feel some wool, our hair. Work out how many sunrises there have been since they were born.

Everything that we know and make, here in our exciting and beautiful universe, comes from something God has made. If we look carefully we can see God's love all around us in the things he has made. Look at all the objects again, helping the children to see how the great big sky over all of us is like the great big love God has for all of us. In the rosehip and the peapod we can see the loving way that God is careful with all the little things as well as the huge things. Each tiny seed and pea, each tiny baby, young child and little old woman is important to God.

God's love shines in our lives and warms our hearts, just as the sun shines on our bodies and warms us. The rain shows us how God showers us with blessings and happiness, without check-ing up first on how good we have been. And just as the sun rises day after day after day, so God is faithful and reliable, and we know we can trust him.

Praying

Your love is deeper than the sea
and wider than the sky.
You shower us with love
like you shower us with your rain –
lots and lots and lots of it!
The warm sun is just like
the warmth of your love.
And day after day after day
you forgive us
again and again and again!
Amen.

God's Beautiful World (2)

Words from the Bible

Lord, you have made so many things! How wisely you made them all! The earth is filled with your creatures.

Psalm 104:24

Doing and learning

Prepare a selection of smells and textures for the children to sample. Here are some suggestions:

- incense sticks or essential oils of different fragrances
- primroses and daffodils
- fruits and vegetables
- bark, new and crackly leaves, shells, feathers and stones
- different textured fabrics

Gather round all the objects and talk with the children about the ones they specially like, enjoying the variety. We have all been born into this beautiful world, with all its colours and shapes to look at and enjoy. Go through different categories of what there is, so that they can think of examples of them all (for example, round, red, yellow, prickly, shiny, rough and smooth, quiet and loud, quick and slow, little and big, and things that are invisible and hidden). What a loving God it must be who thought of all this and gave us such a lovely planet to live on!

Praying

All that we can hear and everything we
    can see,
including me,
we all of us spring from God,
who cares for each of us unendingly.
Let the whole earth sing of his love!

Caring for God's World

Words from the Bible

Then the Lord God placed the man in the Garden of Eden to cultivate it and guard it.   *Genesis 2:15*

Doing and learning

Scatter around some fallen leaves. The children gather them up one at a time and bring them to place them on brown, red, orange, yellow or green paper, matching the leaf to the approximate colour of the paper.

Talk about the lovely colours of our world in all the different seasons, and show them different coloured pieces of paper. What do the colours remind them of? (The blue of sky and sea and forget-me-nots, the pink of sunsets and roses, and so on.) Celebrate the colourful world God has made.

When God made people, he gave us an important job to do. We are to look after this world, and all the universe, as carefully as we possibly can. We are to look after the ground (place down a chunk of rock) and all the minerals of our planet like gold and silver, iron and copper, calcium and sulphur. We are to look after all the growing plants (place down a potted plant) like rain forests and cactus, fruits, flowers and herbs. We are to look after all the animals (place down a book of animals and turn through some of the pages) like horses, fish, birds, spiders and worms.

And we are to look after one another (place down a book with pictures of people from all different parts of the world and flick through it), sharing so that everyone has enough to eat, and taking care of one another.

Are there any children who are ready to help God look after the world? That's good! Could we start today? How? Talk over their ideas and do your best to put into practice any that are practical. (What about giving each child a bag to collect litter in and cleaning up this patch of the world together? Or recycling their newspapers, bottles, stamps and cans?) Scribe the ideas and put them in the church magazine.

Praying

Father God, we love this world
that you have made.
We are old enough to help look after it
and we're going to start by . . .

Thank You, God

Words from the Bible

Every day I will thank you; I will praise you for ever and ever.   *Psalm 145:2*

Doing and learning

Sit in a circle and pass round a paper plate or a broom stick. Each person mimes with the object to show what it is. (Examples might be a steering wheel or a fishing rod.)

Point out how we managed to say what the plate or stick was, using not words but actions. In the circle try out some more telling actions, such as showing by our faces that we're pleased or grumpy, interested or scared.

Today we are going to look at some of the ways we can say 'thank you' to God for making us and such a lovely world, for forgiving us and looking after us.

We can say our thanks to God. Go round the circle with the children who want to thank God for different things.

We can silently say our thanks to God. Suggest everyone shuts their eyes and puts their hands together, as we all thank God silently for something or someone special to us.

We can sing and shout and dance our thanks to God! Play and sing a favourite praise song, with the children singing along, dancing and playing instruments.

So we can tell God our thanks by saying aloud, saying silently, singing, shouting, dancing and playing . . . *and* by living our thanks.

How do we live our thanks?

Well, if we want to tell God how happy we are that he has made a lovely world, we can show him our thanks by being careful to look after it. (Chat together about ways this might be done.)

If we want to tell God how happy we are that he has given us loving people to look after us, we can show him our thanks by being helpful to those people. (Again, talk over examples.)

If we want to tell God how happy we are that he forgives us when we do things wrong, we can show him our thanks by forgiving other people.

Praying

Father God, we want to thank you
for your loving kindness,
and to show you that we thank you
we will live our thanks each day.
Watch our living and you will see
how loving and kind we'll try to be!
Amen.

THE STORY OF JESUS

God's Message of Love

Words from the Bible

And God showed his love for us by sending his only Son into the world.

1 John 4:9

Doing and learning

Collect some model cars and trucks (sized to suit the children in your group) and sit everyone down, spread out. Let them whizz the cars from one to another across the spaces.

Talk about how we can send a car off to reach a friend (demonstrate with one car to a child on the other side of the circle) and they can send it back to us. We do the same thing with messages. I can think to myself, 'Mmm, I'd like to thank the children for putting the cars away so nicely', and all I have to do is say the words out loud (say them out loud) and the message races across to your ears! Hands up if you caught the message. Clever, isn't it?

(You could have one or two children sending out a message, and the rest of you catching the spoken message with your ears.)

You can't see those messages, can you? But you can hear them. Some messages you *can* see. What's this one? (Show the road sign for a school.) And this? (Show a green man sign.) That time you caught the message with your eyes.

At Christmas God sent us a very important message. The message looked like this. (Show a picture of the Nativity.) And it meant this. (Show a red heart with the words 'I love you' on it, and read them out.)

Jesus is God's message of love. Jesus is God saying, 'I love you!' (All join in.)

Praying

Dear God, I am glad
that you love us so much.
It makes me happy!
Amen.

Born in Bethlehem

Words from the Bible

'This very day in David's town your Saviour was born – Christ the Lord!'

Luke 2:11

Doing and learning

Have a cardboard crown and put it on one of the children who then leads the others to do whatever they do (follow my leader). Swap the crown over till everyone who wants to has a turn at being king or queen.

Put the crown on one child's head, and a kingly robe round their shoulders. Once there was a famous king of Israel called King David. He loved God and was a very good king. King David had been born in a city you might have heard of. It was the city of Bethlehem! King David was not brought up in a palace. (Take out a toy sheep and hold it.) He was brought up as a shepherd boy on the hills near Bethlehem, where he helped to look after the sheep. He grew up strong and good, and looking after the people as their king.

(Get out a shiny star, and take the crown from King David. Place the star, the crown and the sheep on the floor together.) Many years later another baby was born in the city of Bethlehem who would grow up to be a king and a shepherd. Do you know what his name was? It was Jesus! (Place a Christmas card or picture showing the Nativity on the floor with the other things.) And as we get ready for Christmas we are getting ready to welcome Jesus, the baby king, who was born into our world at King David's city of Bethlehem.

Praying

Lord Jesus, my King,
(bow head)
to you I will bring
(kneel down)
my living, my loving,
(arms out, palms up, then hands on heart)
and every good thing!
(arms stretched up, hands open)

The Shepherds Visit Jesus

Words from the Bible

There were some shepherds in that part of the country who were spending the night in the fields, taking care of their flocks.   *Luke 2:8*

Doing and learning

Have a crib scene set up somewhere in the room, and dress one child up as an angel. Talk about going to visit people at Christmas – perhaps some of them got in a car or went on a bus or train to visit family or friends, or perhaps some of them had visitors coming to see them. Were there any babies in the places they went?

Today we are going to look at some of the visitors the baby Jesus had, soon after he was born.

In a circle, pretend you are all shepherds, sitting out on the hills under the night sky, round a warm fire. Wrap your cloaks around you, and warm your hands at the fire, getting nice and close to keep cosy. All around us the sheep are bleating. (All make some faraway and nearby bleats.) Look up at all the stars and try to count them . . . oh, there are too many to count, but isn't it beautiful to see the stars shining!

But what's that light in the sky? It's so bright, and it seems to be all around us! (All shrink away from the light, putting your hands up to shield your eyes.) And there's an angel, here on our ordinary hillside! (The child dressed as an angel comes and stands near the group, arms raised.)

The angel said to the shepherds, 'Don't be afraid!' (The angel says, 'Don't be afraid!') All start to relax a bit and get ready to listen to the angel's message. Go into narrative mode and explain that the angel told the shepherds that he had some wonderful news to tell them. A Saviour has just been born in their town of Bethlehem, and they are invited to go and visit him. They'll find him easily because he's wrapped up and lying in the straw in a stable.

The shepherds all look at one another with their eyes open wide in surprise. Just then lots of other angels fill the sky all around them (all look up and point at them), and they're all singing God's praises for all they're worth! (We could all join in – 'Glory to God, glory to God, glory to the Father.')

Then the brightness started to fade away, and the shepherds were sitting in the starry night, rubbing their eyes to make sure they weren't dreaming. But they all remembered the light and the angels and the singing, didn't they? (All look at one another, agreeing.)

Now you're back to being a shepherd again. Suggest that you all go and see if you can find this baby who is God's Son. In a stable in Bethlehem, didn't the angel say? Are we ready, then? (Lead the group of shepherds across to the crib and kneel around it.)

Praying

Jesus, like the shepherds,
we want to welcome you
and thank you for being born.
We love you, Jesus!
Amen.

The Wise Men Follow a Star

Words from the Bible

'We saw his star when it came up in the east, and we have come to worship him.'

Matthew 2:2

Doing and learning

Fix a star on to a stick and give it to one of the children. Wherever this child goes with the star, the others follow. If the star stops, everyone stops. Swap the star around until everyone who wants to lead has had a go.

On a long strip of lining paper or wallpaper draw some hills and a starry sky, based on the picture below. Lay the sheet out in front of the children, and have at the ready a shiny star and a cut-out picture of the wise men. The smaller you make these the longer the journey will look.

Who do we know who followed a star? Yes, it was the wise men from many miles away. They followed a great bright star in the sky which was moving, night by night. (Move the star as you speak, and then make the wise men walk after it to catch it up.) The star went on like this for nights and nights, until at last it stopped. (Stop the star over the town of Bethlehem.) And the wise men followed it all the way to a town called Bethlehem. Who did they find at Bethlehem? They found Jesus there. (Place a Christmas card of Joseph, Mary and Jesus on the city of Bethlehem.)

What did they do when they found Jesus? (Swap the Christmas card for one showing the wise men giving their presents.) They treated Jesus as if he was a little king. They bowed and knelt in front of him, and gave him the presents they had brought.

What were the presents? There was gold (lay down something gold – preferably real gold if practical! If you are wearing a gold ring you can take it off and place it down, which says a lot about real giving without a word spoken) . . . frankincense (again the real thing is ideal, so they can smell what it's like) . . . and myrrh (the Body Shop sells it, or use any spicy ointment and let them rub a bit into their skin if they want to).

Praying

Jesus, can you guess
(pretend to hide a present behind your back)
what I have brought
to give you?
It's ME!
(bring hands out and hold them up and out, as you jump forward)

Jesus and the Fishermen

Words from the Bible

As Jesus walked along the shore of Lake Galilee, he saw two fishermen, Simon and his brother Andrew, catching fish with a net.   *Mark 1:16*

Doing and learning

Play the fishing game, using either a commercial version or a homemade one – coloured paper fish with paperclips, and pea-stick fishing rods with string lines and opened paperclip hooks. Use a (dry) paddling pool, scatter the fish in it and stand each rod in a wellie. The children can hook the fish and throw them back in.

Jesus lived beside a big lake which had lots of fish in it. That meant there were fishing boats, and fishermen who went and caught fish to sell. Invite the children to be fishermen, and do all the actions of mending the nets so there aren't any big holes, and scrubbing the boat out to keep it clean. Then they have to push the boat off from the shore, wade out and climb in the boat, hoist the sail and steer the boat. They let down the anchor, throw the fishing nets out into the water and wait. Then when the net is full of fish they haul the heavy net in, tip the fish into baskets at the bottom of the boat and sail back to the shore. They jump out of the boat and haul it up the beach. Then they have to carry the baskets full of fish to sell in the market. After all that they can lie down and have a bit of a rest while they listen to a story!

One morning Jesus was walking along the beach. He was looking for some people to help him in his work, and he saw the fishermen. Some of them were throwing their nets into the water. (And we know how to do that, don't we?) Some of them were sitting on the beach mending their nets. (And we know how to do that, don't we?)

And Jesus thought fishermen, who are good at catching fish, would be just the people he needed to reach people for God. Fishermen who mended their nets would be just the people he needed to mend people through God's love. So he called them to follow him. 'Follow me!' he said.

And the fishermen were happy to follow Jesus and work with him.

Praying

If I was a fisherman
   (mime fishing)
and Jesus called me,
   (cup hand to ear)
I'd throw down my fishing nets
   (do that)
and run to his side.
   (run on the spot)
I am a child and Jesus calls me.
   (point to yourself, and cup hand to ear)
I say, 'Here I am!'
   (shout it, waving at the same time)
and run to his side.
   (run on the spot)

The Servant King

Words from the Bible

'I am among you as one who serves.'

Luke 22:27

Doing and learning

Yes, your majesty. You will need a small handbell. One child is the king (or queen) and wears a crown. The others are all the king's servants, and they do all the work at the palace. Whenever the king rings his bell, the servants have to run up to where he is and bow or curtsey. Then the king gives his command (with the leader's help) and the servants rush about doing what he says. A leader takes the king to different parts of the palace for ringing the bell. Commands are household jobs, such as 'Sweep the floor!', 'Make the bed!', 'Clean the windows!' and 'Peel the potatoes!'

Put down the crown, and a dustpan and brush. Hold the appropriate symbol as you refer to kings and servants. What is a king? A king is the person who rules over a land and is in charge of it. (We're thinking about traditional, storybook kings here, as this is in keeping with the imagery Jesus uses.) He's the one who gives the orders and tells everyone else what to do. He knows he is powerful and expects everyone to bow or curtsey to him, and say, 'Yes, your majesty!' to him. (The children can try that out, with another child wearing the crown and strutting about importantly.)

What is a servant? They are the ones who do the work, looking after the king and his family, and making sure he has all the things he needs. The servants cook and clean, and do the washing, and tidy up, and buy the food, and weed the garden, and clean out the gerbils, and put out the rubbish, and polish the tables, and scrape mud off the shoes . . . ! (The children can try all these out in quick succession, till everyone is out of breath.)

Who would they rather be – the king or a servant?

Now Jesus is our King, but he isn't anything like the sort of king we've been talking about, is he? It's true he is very important. It's true he is powerful and reigns over us all. But Jesus came into our world as a tiny baby, living in an ordinary family, like ours, without any palace or power. He worked as an ordinary carpenter, making things out of wood. In fact, Jesus is a king, but he behaves like a servant! He went around looking after people, making them better and cheering them up. He looks after us now, helping us wherever we need help.

(Put the crown over the dustpan and brush.) So Jesus is both a king *and* a servant, not bossing us around but caring for us all because he loves us.

Praying

Leader: We pray for kings and queens and presidents and everyone in charge.
All: Lord, make them wise and good.
Leader: We pray for those who clean and cook and everyone not in charge.
All: Lord, make them wise and good.
Leader: Our Servant King, we pray for each other.
All: Lord, make us wise and good. Amen.

Jesus on a Donkey

Words from the Bible

Jesus found a donkey and rode on it, just as the scripture says, 'Do not be afraid, city of Zion! Here comes your King, riding on a young donkey.'

John 12:14-15

Doing and learning

Pin the tail on the donkey. Use a picture of a donkey and make a tail from some wool, with blutack on the top end. The children shut their eyes (or have them blindfolded) and fix the tail where they reckon it belongs. Using an old sock and some wool they can make a donkey puppet to remind them of today's teaching. (If you don't have any old socks, try the charity shops, or a jumble sale.)

There's a donkey in our story today. He was just an ordinary donkey, and a young one, but he was given a very important job to do.

Tell the children the story of Jesus' entry into Jerusalem from the donkey's point of view. Bring in what the donkey saw and heard and felt and smelt, and how pleased and proud he felt to have his friend Jesus riding on his back. If you prefer to have a 'script', Palm Tree Bible Stories have it written from the donkey's perspective in *Jesus on a donkey*, and Nan Goodall's classic, *Donkey's glory* (Mowbray, 1980), includes this special journey.

Praying

(Jingle some keys or bottle tops during this prayer.)

Donkey riding, donkey riding,
hear the children sing!
Donkey riding, donkey riding,
'JESUS IS OUR KING!'

Easter Day

Words from the Bible

'The Son of man must be handed over to sinful men, be crucified, and three days later rise to life.'   *Luke 24:7*

Doing and learning

Hide some Easter eggs (outside if possible) and have an Easter egg hunt before distributing them fairly among the children.

Look together at some hens' eggs and pictures of chicks, birds and dinosaurs, all coming from eggs. Talk about the springtime and all the signs of new life around at the moment.

Today is Easter Day. It's very special because it's the day we remember Jesus coming to life for ever. Jesus went around doing good and loving people, making them better and helping them get to know what God is like. But some people wanted Jesus out of the way, and he was killed – they nailed him to a big cross. It was very sad, but Jesus went on loving and forgiving even then.

When some of his friends went to the grave on the Sunday morning, they couldn't find his dead body; it wasn't there. Why? Because Jesus wasn't dead any more – he was alive! He would never die again. Jesus is alive for ever! (You could all sing *Jesus' love is very wonderful* to celebrate.)

Praying

Did Jesus die? YES!
Is Jesus dead? NO!
Is he alive again? YES, YES, YES!
JESUS IS ALIVE!

Jesus Goes to Heaven

Words from the Bible

As he was blessing them, he departed from them and was taken up into heaven.

Luke 24:51

Doing and learning

Hello, goodbye. As the music plays, the children skip and jump about. When it stops, they find another person, shake hands and say, 'Hello'. As the music starts again, they wave and say, 'Goodbye', before skipping and jumping off somewhere else.

Our lives are full of hellos and goodbyes. Share some of the times we say hello and goodbye. Sometimes the goodbyes can be sad, if we've been with a special friend, or grandparents, and have to say goodbye to them. We know that means we won't be seeing them for a while.

Jesus' friends had got used to him being there to talk and laugh with. They loved being with Jesus. Even when Jesus had risen from the dead he would spend time with them sometimes. But now Jesus took his friends out to a hill and told them it was time to say goodbye. They wouldn't be seeing him any more as it was time for him to go back to heaven.

But Jesus wasn't going to leave his friends all alone. He loved them! He promised that in a few days he would send them a special present. When the present came they would be able to feel Jesus there with them all the time. That made the friends happy. They watched as a cloud took Jesus up out of their sight, and then they went back to Jerusalem to wait for the special present.

Praying

Be near me, Lord Jesus, I ask thee to stay close by me for ever and love me, I pray.
Bless all the dear children in thy tender care,
and fit us for heaven to live with thee there.

JESUS AND US

Discovering Jesus

Words from the Bible

Jesus turned, saw them following him, and asked, 'What are you looking for?'
John 1:38

Doing and learning

A treasure trail in pictures. Prepare simple drawings of different places in the room and number them. Keep number 1 yourself, and place number 2 in the place shown on number 1. Continue placing all the pictures until at the last place (pictured in the previous number) you put the treasure – enough sweets/stickers/crayons for everyone. Start off by showing everyone the first picture, which sends them off to where the second one is lurking, and so on until they are led to the treasure.

Talk about how we were led to the treasure bit by bit, and not straight-away. Each clue led us a little closer.

What things can help us to find out who Jesus is?

Have a candle, some water and a toy sheep all hidden separately under cloths or tea towels. Explain that hidden here we've got some things which can lead us to find out who Jesus is and what he is like.

Uncover the candle. What can a candle tell us about Jesus? Light the candle as you explain that a candle is a living flame of light in the darkness; it helps us see, so we don't trip over things, and it shows things up clearly. And that's what Jesus does. He is the light of love and goodness shining in the darkness of all that is wrong and bad. He helps us see the right way to live so we don't waste our lives hating and spoiling.

Uncover the water. What can water tell us about Jesus? Water is clear and clean, it washes, and when we are thirsty it takes our thirst away. And that's what Jesus does. We can always trust him because he is always honest with us, he forgives us when we are sorry for making others unhappy, and he is like a drink when you're thirsty – very nice!

Uncover the sheep. What can a sheep tell us about Jesus? Sheep need a shepherd, and so do we. Jesus is like a good shepherd who looks after us and leads us safely through our whole life.

Praying

Left, right, left, right,
we are walking your way, Jesus.
Left, right, left, right,
that's the way to go!
Left, right, left, right,
we are walking your way, Jesus.
Left, right, left, right,
Let the loving show!

Jesus Is Here

Words from the Bible

The doors were locked, but Jesus came and stood among them and said, 'Peace be with you.'   *John 20:26*

Doing and learning

Have four different sounds, such as a bell, a drum, a rattle and a whistle. When the children hear the sounds they do the appropriate actions. The bell means 'now clap', the drum 'now jump up and down', the rattle 'now sit', and the whistle 'now smile'.

Talk about what we are all doing now. This might be sitting in a circle, listening, folding our arms, breathing, and thinking. Some things, like breathing, we do all the time, and hardly notice. Take a few breaths to notice what goes on day and night, when we're awake and when we're asleep, so that we stay alive. So there's lots going on *now* just in our own body.

What's going on now as well as us sitting in a circle in St Martin's, East Ham? Lots of other groups of children are sitting in their circles in other churches! (Why not pray for them now – they will be praying for you!) What else is going on now? Think about what is happening at the moment on the roads and in hospitals, and in other countries, where some people are fast asleep and others are going to bed.

We only see our little bit of *now*, but God sees all of it! Jesus is here *now* for all the people and all the places!

Praying

(Loudly) Tick tock, tick tock,
Jesus you are with us NOW!
(Softly) Tick tock, tick tock,
(Very softly) Jesus . . . you are here.

Don't Be Afraid

Words from the Bible

'Do not be afraid,' Jesus said to them.
Matthew 28:10

'Don't be afraid,' Jesus told them, 'it is I!'
John 6:20

Doing and learning

What's the time, Mr Wolf? The children creep up on Mr Wolf, asking him the time, and he replies with different times. If he says, 'Dinner time!' the children turn and run as Mr Wolf tries to catch someone.

Talk about how mums and dads make us feel safe when we're scared or frightened. Sometimes they make us laugh and show us that we don't need to be frightened. (Like Dad pretending to wear a bib, so the baby sees it as funny instead of scary.) Sometimes they explain so we aren't scared any more because we understand it better. (Like barking being a dog's way of saying hello.) And if something really is frightening, mums and dads make us feel safer just by holding us close to them, or just being there. (You can use parent and baby soft toys to act out these situations.)

Now explain that God is like that with us all. When his disciples were all scared, on the first Easter Day, or in a storm at sea, Jesus came and comforted them. Jesus knows when we're scared, and we can tell him all about it. He will help us to be brave. He works through other people to look after us, and he works through us to look after other people who are scared. So whenever we make someone feel better, or calm their fears, we are working on God's team!

Praying

I will lie down in peace
and sleep;
it is you, Lord,
who keeps me safe.
Amen.

The Peace of Jesus

Words from the Bible

'Peace is what I leave with you; it is my own peace that I give you. I do not give it as the world does. Do not be worried and upset; do not be afraid.' *John 14:27*

Praying

Give me your peace,
O Jesus Christ, my brother,
give me your peace,
O Jesus Christ, my Lord!

Doing and learning

Bring either a small parachute or a large sheet and stand everyone around the outside, holding the edge. They can now make a flat calm, then build up through very gentle ripples to a full-blown storm, before making it die down again, ending with a gentle peace.

Talk about what happens when we're frightened and about the people who calm us down and make us feel better. Also talk about any people and pets we calm down and comfort, when they're feeling frightened or worried.

Jesus is like that. When we are frightened or scared or upset, whether we're children or grown-ups, we can all come to Jesus and he will help to calm us down and comfort us. He may do that through your family, and he may use *your* words and arms to comfort other people or other creatures!

Sometimes you will find that as you ask Jesus to help you calm down, you will suddenly feel inside like our sheet was at the end of our pretend storm – all gentle and peaceful. Jesus is very good at bringing us peace, and all we have to do is ask for his help.

The Good Shepherd

Words from the Bible

'I am the good shepherd. As the Father knows me and I know the Father, in the same way I know my sheep and they know me. And I am willing to die for them.'   *John 10:14-15*

Doing and learning

Hunt the sheep. Use a soft toy sheep and take it in turns to hide it while everyone closes their eyes. Then everyone looks for it until it's found again.

The children can help you make a landscape of hills, using a large towel draped over some upturned pots and basins, and arranging a few pot plants on it. Wind a long blue scarf between the hills as a stream of water. Place some sheep on the hills. These can either be model or toy ones, or they can be made from the pattern below.

Move the sheep around (the children can make all the sheep and lamb bleating noises) as you tell them how a good shepherd looks after the sheep, taking them to places where there is plenty of grass to eat, leading them to the water so they can drink, and making sure they are safe from howling wolves and growling bears. A good shepherd loves his sheep and knows each of them by name, and he'll never leave them in danger, even if it means getting hurt himself.

Explain that Jesus talks about himself as being like our Good Shepherd. (Move the sheep around as you talk about God's care of us.) He looks after us and loves us, and knows each of us by name. (Mention each of the children and leaders' names.)

Praying

The Lord is my Shepherd,
> *(hold each finger in turn, so the ring finger is held on 'my')*

there is nothing else I need.
> *(keep holding ring finger and shake head)*

Friends of Jesus

Words from the Bible

'I do not call you servants any longer, because a servant does not know what his master is doing. Instead, I call you friends because I have told you everything I have heard from my Father.'

John 15:15

Doing and learning

Have an assortment of toys to play with, so that everyone can enjoy playing together as friends.

Talk together about friends. Friends play together, giggle together and chat together. Friends stick up for one another and share things. Friends like being with each other. What do some of the children like about their friends? (Pass a soft toy around. This is held by the person who is talking, and the others listen.)

We are friends of Jesus. Jesus likes being with us and chatting with us, listening to our news and all the sad as well as the happy things. And he's always there for us – he doesn't suddenly go off us and not like us any more.

What do friends of Jesus do? They love one another, just as Jesus loves them.

Praying

Jesus, you are our friend and we are
    yours.
In all we think and speak and do
    *(point to head, mouth and then open
    hands)*
help us to love one another.
    (spread arms wide)
Amen.

Jesus' Family

Words from the Bible

Jesus said to them all, 'My mother and brothers are those who hear the word of God and obey it.'   *Luke 8:21*

Doing and learning

Part of the family. Stand in a circle. Tell each group in turn the way to move in the circle, like this: 'If you are a brother, run in the circle; if you are a sister, skip round the circle; if you have an uncle, stand still in the circle; if you have a grandma, walk about in the circle.'

Talk about the way we look a bit like other people in our family, and look for family likenesses in children from the same family, or with families everyone in the group knows well. Sometimes we are alike in the way we look and sometimes in how we walk, fiddle with our fingers, or laugh. Sometimes we are like other people in our family in being quiet or noisy, losing our temper or liking music.

One day Jesus was sitting talking to a circle of his friends, rather like we are sitting now. Someone told him that his mother, brothers and sisters were outside. Jesus looked around at all the people and told them he thought of everyone living God's way as part of his close family!

So that means us as well. We are part of Jesus' family, and when we are living God's way we're showing the family likeness.

Praying

(To the tune of *Twinkle, twinkle, little star*)

Jesus, Jesus, can I be
in your loving family?
When I live the loving way,
loving others every day,
Jesus, Jesus, I can be
in your loving family!

THE CHRISTIAN LIFE

Baptism

Words from the Bible

'Go, then, to all peoples everywhere and make them my disciples: baptise them in the name of the Father, the Son, and the Holy Spirit.'   *Matthew 28:19*

Doing and learning

Have a time of water play. To cut down on mess, protect the floor with plastic sheeting (plastic tablecloths are good for this job) and have several washing-up bowls with a lowish level of water in them. Gather an assortment of containers, tea strainers and funnels to play with.

Talk about playing in the water at a swimming pool, on the beach or by a river, and what the water looks, sounds and feels like. What is it like under the water? What happens to dirty things when they're washed in water?

When people promise to spend their life following Jesus, they are washed in water in church, and given their name. It's called being baptised, or Christened. (Talk about the font in your church, and any baptisms they remember, and show some pictures of people being baptised.)

When Jesus was baptised in the river Jordan, he waded into the water and John the Baptist (who was Jesus' cousin) dipped him right under the water. When he came up, all wet, he heard God, his Father, saying to him, 'You are my Son and I love you. I am very pleased with you.'

Praying

Lord God,
I am one of your children.
I belong to you!
Amen.

The Holy Spirit Comes

Words from the Bible

They were all filled with the Holy Spirit.

Acts 2:4

Doing and learning

Pass the parcel. Beforehand prepare an outline picture based on the one below.

Cut flame shapes from coloured paper to fit exactly over the flames in the picture. Pack the flames into the layers of the parcel and the silhouettes of the disciples' heads in the 'prize' place. You can add a sweet if you wish! As each flame is unwrapped the child sticks it on to the right space, until the group has collectively completed the whole picture.

Today we are celebrating! It's rather like the birthday of the Church, because today we remember how Jesus sent the Holy Spirit on his friends so they would be filled with God's love and power.

What did the Holy Spirit sound like? It sounded like a strong wind, blowing round the house. (All make the sound.)

What did the Holy Spirit look like? It looked like flames of fire. (Light twelve tea-light candles.)

What did the Holy Spirit feel like? It felt like being happy and excited and peaceful all at once, and wanting to tell everyone about how lovely it is to be loved by God.

Praying

Come, Holy Spirit,
and fill me up with God's love.
I may be small
and not very tall
but I can be BIG with God's love!
(Make yourself as big as possible)

The Cost of Love

Words from the Bible

'The greatest love a person can have for his friends is to give his life for them.'

John 15:13

Doing and learning

Play shops, with cartons, fruit and vegetables for sale and toy money, so that they get the idea of there being cost and payment.

Talk about their shopping, and bring out a carrier bag from a local supermarket, with some cheap and expensive items in it. Talk together about which don't cost very much, and which cost a lot. Mention other things which cost lots and lots of money, like houses and holidays. We have to save up for things like that. Sometimes we see a toy or a game we would like, but we don't think it's worth all the money, so we choose not to get it. (Or Mum and Dad say that!)

There was something that Jesus wanted very, very much. It wasn't a toy, and it wasn't something to eat or wear. What Jesus really wanted was to save the world. He wanted us all to be happy and free. But how much would it cost? It couldn't be bought with money. It could only be bought with his life.

Jesus thought about it. He wondered if it was really worth giving up his life so we could be happy and free. He knew that giving up his life would hurt. A lot.

But remember, Jesus loves us very much. He loves us so much that he decided he was even willing to give up his life so we could be free and happy. He thought it was worth the cost of all

that hurt. So he did it, and that's why we can be happy and free!

Praying

(Sing this to the tune of *Frère Jacques*, with the children echoing the leader's words and actions.)

I am dancing, **I am dancing,**
  (dance)
'Thank you, God!' **'Thank you, God!'**
  (clap hands)
I am singing, **I am singing,**
  (sway)
'Thank you, God!' **'Thank you, God!'**
  (clap hands)

Learning to Trust

Words from the Bible

I trust in his constant love for ever and ever.   *Psalm 52:8*

Doing and learning

Sit in a circle and show the children the items mentioned as you ask them to decide which of the two they would trust:

- Which would you trust to sit on – a chair or a balloon?

- Which would you trust to build a house with – bricks or sponges?

- Which would you trust to swing on – cotton or a rope?

- Which would you choose to carry your packed lunch in – an airtight box or an envelope?

We trust things that we think will work well – things that won't let us down. And we trust people who love us, because we know they will be wanting us to be safe and happy. We can't trust strangers, because we don't know if they are wanting us to be safe and happy or not. Use a parent and a child puppet to act this out. First the child is scared of riding a new bike, but the parent re-assures them that they will be holding them so they will be safe. The child agrees to try, as the parent has promised to make sure they don't fall. Then the child wants to ride on the main road, but the parent explains they can't because it's too dangerous. The child reluctantly agrees, knowing that the parent is wanting them to be safe because they are loved.

God is like a loving parent to all of us – God loves us and wants us to be safe and happy for always, in this life and after we die. So we can trust God completely. He will never do anything bad or wrong. He will never let us down. He is always there, watching over us and loving us.

Praying

Jesus, we know we can trust you –
you love us
and will never let us down.
Amen.

Listening

Words from the Bible

'But when you pray, go to your room, close the door, and pray to your Father, who is unseen.'   *Matthew 6:6*

Doing and learning

Explain that you are going to do a spot of listening today. Give out to the children pictures or models of different animals. Ask them all to shout to you the name of their animal or the noise it makes, and you will listen to what they are telling you. Finding that very hard, ask them instead to tell you one by one, so that you can hear them better.

Point out how much easier it is to listen when we are quiet and still, without lots of other noises going on. One of the ways we pray to God is by making ourselves very quiet and still, so that we can listen to God's love, and feel him close to us.

Try being very quiet and still and listening for a pin to drop. Then try being still and quiet, with eyes closed (they can lie face down for this if they like), while you read this to them:

Imagine you are walking along beside a high wall and you see a little door in it. Over the door there is a picture of you and your name is written there. You turn the handle and the door opens. You walk inside and find a sunny day with soft green grass under your feet, and flowers growing there. You feel happy and safe in this place, and take off your shoes and run across the grass, enjoying the coloured flowers and the butterflies. You come to a sandy beach, and the sea is lapping against it, so you sit down and listen to the waves. Although you can't see him, you know that Jesus is here with you, and you sit quietly in the sunshine together by the sea, with the seagulls calling.

After a while you get up and walk back across the beach and the grass, put on your shoes and make your way to the door. As you go out of the door you know that you can come back to this garden of prayer whenever you like.

(Put on some very quiet music as you tell the children to sit up slowly and open their eyes. Pray today's prayer together while the music plays.)

Praying

O Jesus, we love to be with you!
Thank you so much for being our
    special friend,
always here with us and always
    loving us.
Amen.

Speaking

Words from the Bible

'A good person brings good out of the treasure of good things in his heart; a bad person brings bad out of his treasure of bad things. For the mouth speaks what the heart is full of.'   *Luke 6:45*

Doing and learning

Tongue twisters. Try saying some of these: 'She sells sea shells on the sea shore'; 'red lorry, yellow lorry'; 'thirty thousand feathers on a thrush's throat'.

Our tongues are very useful for talking. There are lots of sounds we can only make if we use our tongues – like ddd, ttt, nnn, ng, kkk, lll, sss. They can try making these sounds, noticing where their tongues go. Talking is a wonderful skill to have, and we start learning how to do it as soon as we are born. (Perhaps some of them have baby brothers and sisters who are just beginning to say the odd word.)

So now that we have learnt how to use our tongues for talking, what can we do with our talking? We can ask for exactly what we want or need, instead of crying and hoping someone will understand. We can tell other people what we are thinking. We can tell jokes. We can chat to our friends and we can pray to Jesus. We can cheer people up. We can help other people by telling them how to do something. (They can think of examples for all of these.) Put down a happy face and point out that we can use our tongues for saying all kinds of good and useful things.

Is that the only way we can use our tongues in talking? No, we could choose to use our tongues to say nasty, unkind things, or to be rude and disobedient, or to tell lies, or make someone cry. (Show an unhappy face.) But what a waste of a good tongue that would be. God has given us a wonderful gift of speaking. Let's use that gift to make the world a happier place.

Praying

Chatter, chatter, chatter,
thank you, God, for tongues to talk with,
tongues to tell the truth with,
tongues to speak kind words with,
tongues to pray and tongues to say,
chatter, chatter, chatter!

Caring

Words from the Bible

Help to carry one another's burdens, and in this way you will obey the law of Christ.   *Galatians 6:2*

Doing and learning

Think of someone in the church community who would appreciate receiving a special 'get well soon' card from the children's group (or whatever the need is). Explain this to the children and bring a suitable card along. Give each child a small piece of paper on which to draw a message, write the children's names on their drawings and stick them all into the card. The children can help put the card into its envelope and see it addressed and stamped.

The children have done a very kind thing this morning, and that card will certainly cheer someone up. God loves to see us looking after one another's needs like that. It makes him very happy indeed!

Jesus always noticed what people were wanting, and went out of his way to help them. If he saw that someone was sad and lonely he would go and talk to them. When people came to him with their legs or backs not working, Jesus loved to mend their bodies and put them right. Jesus calls all his followers (and that's *us*!) to do the same thing – to look after one another's needs.

So how can we do that? What kind things could we do? Talk over their ideas and write them down. (It doesn't matter that they can't read them; they can see that you think they are important.) Read the list of suggestions back to them and give each of them a secret sign on their hand and your own (draw a smiley face) to remind you all of the kind things you and God are planning to do together. Suggest they do them as a secret between them and God.

The children can do another kind thing by making a scrap book of pictures and prayers to be passed around among those who would enjoy such a book. Provide a scrap book and some pictures for the children to cut out and stick in, and scribe for each child so that their prayers are also included.

Praying

Father God, we want to pray
for those who are sad or lonely,
for those who are ill,
for those who are very busy
and get tired from all their jobs.
Please help us to help them.
Amen.

Sharing

Words from the Bible

'There is a boy here who has five loaves of barley bread and two fish.' *John 6:9*

Doing and learning

Prepare enough different coloured paper shapes for each child in the group to have one of each. There need to be as many different categories as there are children. Give each child a pile of a particular coloured shape so that everyone has a pile. (They can set up their own 'base', or have their shapes in a yoghurt pot.) All the children go round sharing the shapes out until they end up with a pile of different ones. These are arranged into a pattern on the floor in front of them.

Admire everyone's patterns and talk about how we have all been sharing what we were given so that we could all make our lovely pictures. Today we are going to hear about a child who offered to share his lunch with Jesus.

Spread out a sheet or bath towel on the floor and sit around it. Place on it some blue material or paper to be a lake, and stand a few plants in pots around as bushes and trees. Place a model boat on the lake. Talk about the landscape you are making as you add the items, and let the children help.

One day Jesus and his friends went over the lake in a boat. All the crowds of people walked round the side of the lake (everyone finger walks), so they could be there when the boat arrived. Jesus climbed out of the boat and taught the people, telling them stories to help them understand how much God loved them.

Soon they were all very hungry, but they were a long way from their homes. One boy had some packed lunch with him. (Produce a packed lunch box.) He could have just sat and eaten it, but he knew the others were hungry too, and he heard Jesus talking to his friends about how to feed all these people.

So he went up to Andrew, one of Jesus' friends.

'Excuse me,' he said, 'but is this any use? There's five barley loaves and two small fish.'

Andrew took the boy and his lunch to Jesus, and Jesus looked very happy and thanked the boy very much for offering to share his food. 'Because you've been so kind, you've given enough here for everyone!' Jesus whispered to the boy. 'Watch carefully!'

Everyone sat down on the grass and Jesus gave thanks for the little lunch; he thanked God for providing enough for everyone, but the boy couldn't think how there would be enough. Jesus started breaking up the bread and the fish, and his friends kept taking it to the groups of people. Somehow the food went on and on, until everyone had eaten as much as they needed. And there was even some left over!

Then let the children make sandwiches, which can be cut up and shared with the rest of the congregation. If you want to be authentic you can have tuna or sardine sandwiches, but other fillings would be fine!

Praying

(This can be prayed before we eat.)
Thank you, God, for food we eat,
that keeps us strong and healthy.
Amen.

Standing Tall

Words from the Bible

'I broke the power that held you down and I let you walk with your head held high.'
Leviticus 26:13

He placed his hands on her, and at once she straightened herself up and praised God.
Luke 13:13

Doing and learning

Choose three different sounds (such as a bell, a shaker and a drum), and a grand, regal piece of music on tape such as *Land of hope and glory*. They move in a different way for each sound – such as crawling, jumping and bunny-hopping – but when the grand music plays they stand up tall and strong, like a good king or queen.

Talk together about behaving well and being good (both adults and children), so that the children are telling you all they know about this. In voicing these good and noble things they will be reinforcing their own expectations of behaviour and beginning to own those values. Don't make any comments which contrast any of this with unacceptable behaviour, or the times we don't do it – we are simply celebrating the good we know about. Talk about how we behave well in different situations, such as in the car, at meal times, when playing with friends, when doing jobs at home. Help them to see that what they are describing is loving behaviour, thinking of other people and being kind and generous, honest and brave. It's Jesus behaviour, and it makes God very happy to see us doing it.

Praying

In your love, Lord Jesus,
I can stand up tall –
do what's right,
do what's good,
live the way I know I should.
In your love, Lord Jesus,
I can stand up tall!
Amen.

God's Armour

Words from the Bible

Put on all the armour that God gives you, so that you will be able to stand up against the Devil's evil tricks.

Ephesians 6:11

Doing and learning

Give the children lots of rolled-up balls of newspaper as snowballs and have either a leader or a child who volunteers to be the one everyone is trying to hit with the paper. However, this person is given a tray as a shield, to protect themselves.

Talk about how much better it was to have the tray as a shield. It really helped to protect the person being pelted with snowballs! Have a look at some other things we use to protect ourselves – overalls and aprons protect our clothes from paint and glue, umbrellas and wet weather clothes protect us from getting too soaked, sunglasses protect our eyes from the glaring sun. If possible, have a look at some toy Roman armour, or a picture of a Roman soldier.

God knows that it isn't always easy to be loving and good, honest and kind. And he knows that sometimes people are hurt by bad things that happen, like wars, or someone being nasty to them, or frightening them, or making them feel silly. God hates to see any of his children getting hurt by any kind of evil, or hurting others. So he gives us armour to protect us from evil.

The armour is God's love, and if we imagine ourselves getting dressed in God's love every day, we'll be wearing his special armour to help us live God's way and fight against evil.

Praying

I am wearing the armour of God
to help me fight against evil.
I am carrying the shield of faith
'cos God wants me to be safe.
Yes, God wants me to be safe and strong,
and I belong to him!

Treasure Pots

Words from the Bible

Yet we who have this spiritual treasure are like common clay pots, in order to show that the supreme power belongs to God, not to us.   *2 Corinthians 4:7*

Doing and learning

Have a number of boxes, pots and tins with a different thing in each. Name one of the objects and let the children guess which container it's in. Open each one to look until you find the right one. With the next object they may have seen it already, so memory as well as guesswork comes into the choosing. Continue till all the objects have been found inside their containers.

Talk about how all those ordinary containers held different treasures. We've got some more containers here today. Count round the number of people present – we've got that number of treasure pots sitting here!

Each of us is like one of those ordinary pots, with secret treasure inside. The treasure is God's great love for us. (Gradually open up a huge red heart of paper.) Wherever we go and whatever we're doing, we know that God loves us, and that treasure makes us very special pots indeed! It means that we can be loving and kind, happy and strong because we haven't just got our loving in us – we've got God's as well.

Praying

I am filled with the love of Jesus –
love in my seeing,
  (point to eyes)
love in my speaking,
  (point to mouth)
love in all I do.
  (open hands)
Thank you, Jesus,
  (raise arms)
your love is ENORMOUS!
  (stretch arms in huge circle)

OLD TESTAMENT STORIES

Noah

Words from the Bible

The Lord said to Noah, 'Go into the boat with your whole family.'   *Genesis 7:1*

Doing and learning

Put stickers of different colours on the children and stand in a circle, holding hands to make archways. When you hold up a colour, the child wearing that colour sticker runs in and out of the archways, round the circle and back to their place. Whenever you hold up a picture of a rainbow, the whole circle joins hands and comes in to the middle and out again, shouting, 'God loves us!'

Spread out carpet tiles or a large sheet on the ground and sit around it. Use cut-outs, based on the pictures below to tell the story of Noah and the flood. Animals can be models if you prefer. The children can help move the characters around. Bring out the way God rescued Noah and his family and kept them safe, and how the rainbow is a sign of God's love that will never let us down.

Praying

(This can be sung to the tune of *One, two, three four five, once I caught a fish alive*)
Violet, indigo and blue –
God loves me, that's always true.
Green, yellow, orange, red –
that is what the rainbow said!

Naaman

Words from the Bible

So Naaman went down to the Jordan, dipped himself in it seven times . . . and he was completely cured.

2 Kings 5:14

Doing and learning

Cut out a number of spots of different colours (about 30 centimetres across) and spread them out on the floor. All round the room are placed small spots of the same colours, and the children go round spotting the spots and placing them on the matching large spot on the floor.

Sometimes we get spots when we're ill. Does anyone remember having spots? (With chicken pox, for instance.) Today we are going to meet someone whose skin was covered in white spots because he had a skin illness. The man's name was Naaman.

Spread out carpet tiles or a couple of large towels on the floor and tell the story from 2 Kings 5:1-14 in your own words, using cut-out pictures of the characters based on the drawings below.

Praying

Dear Father God,
we pray for all the people who are ill,
and for those who are looking after them.
Amen.

Moses and the Manna

Words from the Bible

The people of Israel called the food manna. It was like a small white seed, and tasted like biscuits made with honey.

Exodus 16:31

Doing and learning

Manna? – What is it? Teach the children some Hebrew – that 'manna?' means 'what is it?' and then show them some items, mostly hidden in a bag or by a cloth. As you draw out a bit of a teddy, a jumper or an orange, you say to them, 'Manna?' so they can give the answer – 'It's a teddy!' Then a child can be the person who asks, 'Manna?'

Remind the children, using a Moses basket, a crown, a whip of plaited string and a piece of blue cloth, that Moses was the baby who had been put in a basket and floated down the river to keep him safe when all God's people were slaves in Egypt. He was brought up by Pharaoh's daughter in the palace. When he grew up he had seen how his own people were badly treated as slaves. God used Moses to lead his people out of slavery. They had crossed through the middle of the Red Sea on dry land and now they were travelling in the desert, with Moses leading them.

And they got very hungry, so they all started grumbling. They said, 'It's not fair, Moses! If we were back in Egypt we could be eating nice stews and casseroles.' And they all got very grouchy with Moses.

Moses went off to talk with God about it. 'Lord, they're all moaning and grumbling about not having any food to eat,' he said. 'What should I do?'

God told Moses to let the people know that God knew they needed food and would be getting them some, so the people waited to see what would happen. That evening a flock of quails flew over. Some of the birds couldn't manage to fly any further, and they fell down dead on the ground. So the people picked them up and made a kind of chicken stew with them, and everybody enjoyed it very much.

Next morning there were white flakes all over the ground (scatter some pieces of white paper all over the floor). The people didn't know what it was, so they said to Moses, 'Manna? Manna?' And Moses said, 'This is the food God promised you!' So all the people took bowls (give out little pots) and gathered the white flakes. (The children go and gather it up in their bowls. When they've finished, they sit down again in the story circle.) Explain that our white flakes are just pieces of paper, but the flakes the people gathered up were food which tasted sweet – a bit like honey. And because no one knew what it was really called, they all called it 'manna'.

Using a paper plate the children can make a plate of their favourite food out of playdough. Prepare some brown, green, yellow, red and white – most food can be made from roughly those colours!

Praying

Thank you, God,
for giving us food each day.
Thank you for the farmers who grew it,
the shops that sell it,
and the people who cook it for us!
Amen.

THE ETERNAL KINGDOM

God's Growing Kingdom

Words from the Bible

Jesus went on to say, 'The Kingdom of God is like this. A man scatters seed in his field. He sleeps at night, is up and about during the day, and all the while the seeds are sprouting up, and growing.'

Mark 4:26-27

Doing and learning

Play with very soapy water, making bubbles by blowing through your hands. (Ordinary bubble mix is the rather boring substitute!) As you play, talk about the bubbles growing bigger and bigger, and see who can make the biggest.

How did we make our bubbles grow? We had to blow very carefully and gently. Show the children some little seeds and pictures of what they grow into. Show them some real 'grown' examples as well if this is practical. In the story of Jack and the beanstalk, the beans grew up overnight into a huge plant, but usually the growing goes on bit by bit, day by day, until instead of a tiny seed you find a big tall plant, or even a tree.

Bubbles and plants aren't the only things which grow. *We* grow too! Let them stand up as tall as they can and remember when they were only very short. In the world God has made, there is lots and lots of growing that goes on.

Jesus told his friends one day that, just like the other things that grow, the kingdom of heaven grows and grows. Bit by bit God's love and goodness is growing and spreading. Once there were just a few of Jesus' followers, but now there are friends of Jesus all over the place. We know a few of them, because they are with us in our church. (Name some of them.) Then there are Jesus' friends in all the other churches, not just in this country, but all over the world.

Praying

Pray for each other by name:
Lord Jesus, bless . . . .
Let your love in her/him grow and grow a bit more every day of her/his life.

The Saints in Heaven

Words from the Bible

'People will come from the east and the west, from the north and the south, and sit down at the feast in the Kingdom of God.'   *Luke 13:29*

Doing and learning

Party games. Give everyone a party hat and play a couple of party games such as animal statues. (You tell them which animal to be and when the music stops they freeze in this species. Then they become a new animal.)

We're having quite a party today because we're joining in with all the saints in heaven.

When close friends of Jesus die, that isn't the end of their life. They are welcomed into heaven by Jesus and all the angels, who are very happy to see them. They may have come into heaven tired and worn out from doing lots of good and loving things on earth all through their life, but now all their tiredness goes away and they feel like dancing and singing! They might have known sadness on earth, but when they get to heaven, all their tears are wiped away, and they are filled with happiness and joy instead.

They are really happy to meet their friend Jesus face to face, and it's wonderful to be in all the light and beauty of heaven, where there is nothing nasty or evil, nothing selfish or unkind, but only all that is good and lovely.

All close friends of Jesus will get that welcome in heaven when they die. And the happiness is not just for an afternoon or a week. It lasts for ever and ever and ever!

Continue the party with a few nibbles, and some singing and dancing, praising God.

Praying

Bless all the dear children
in your tender care,
and fit us for heaven
to live with you there.

Everlasting Love

Words from the Bible

. . . his love lasts for ever, and his goodness endures for all generations.

Psalm 103:17

Doing and learning

Give out chocolate buttons to suck and see who can make theirs last the longest.

Some things only last as long as a chocolate button. They are nice to suck but we know they won't last for ever. Bubbles don't last long either. (Blow a few and enjoy their colours and roundness, until they pop.) Lots of good things are with us for just a little while, so it's a good idea to really enjoy them while we have them.

Some things, like long journeys, or grown-up conversations, seem to go on for ages and ages! But even they don't go on for ever. In the end, it's time to get out of the car, or the grown-ups say goodbye and we can carry on walking to the swings.

What will last for ever and ever and ever? To give them a clue, show them a red heart shape. It's *love* that will last for ever, and that's because our God is Love, and God lasts for ever and ever. What kind of loving things do we do? (Share ideas.)

One day, at the end of everything, God will gather up all that goodness and love into his heaven, so it's safe for ever, and not one bit of it will be lost.

Praying

God of love, we thank you
for all the love in our world.
What a good thing that love
lasts for ever and never wears out!

Daniel's Dream

Words from the Bible

And so, in honour of the name of Jesus, all beings in heaven, on earth, and in the world below will fall on their knees, and all will openly proclaim that Jesus Christ is Lord, to the glory of God the Father.   *Philippians 2:10-11*

Doing and learning

Everyone helps decorate the room with paper chains and gold crowns. Then sing and dance to some praise songs, using recorded music such as the *Kid's Praise* albums.

Talk about the dreams we have, and then tell the children the vision of Daniel as a story (in Daniel 7:9-10, 13-14), like this.

Long, long ago there lived a man called Daniel. Daniel worshipped God and tried his best to live God's way. In the days of King Belshazzar, king of Babylon, Daniel had a dream. It was such an amazing dream that he couldn't get it out of his head. Daniel kept thinking about his dream, and in the end he realised that the dream had been given to him by God. So Daniel thought to himself, 'If God has shown me these amazing things in my dream, I expect he wants me to tell all the others about it.'

So Daniel wrote his dream down, and this is it.

'As I looked, I saw a great throne put in its place, and God Almighty sat down on the throne. His clothes were as shining white as snow. His hair was white like sheep's wool. His throne was flaming with fire, blazing and glowing. From the throne there ran a river of fire, pouring out, and burning brightly. Thousands and thousands of people were standing before the throne, as if they were waiting for something. The books were opened.

'Then I saw in front of me what looked like a man. He was coming with the clouds of heaven, closer and closer to Almighty God, and they led him up to the throne. This man was made King over all the people in every place and every time. And as I looked I knew that he would be King for ever and ever and ever.'

That was the dream which Daniel dreamed long, long ago. Long before Jesus had been born. And yet God had shown Daniel a picture of heaven, and he had seen Jesus, coming into heaven and being made King for ever.

Together make a large collage picture of Daniel's dream. Have the outline drawn already (based on the picture below) and bring some shiny flames of fire for the children to stick on to the throne and the fiery river. They can stick wool on to the clouds and coloured tissue paper to the rest of the picture. Call the picture: Daniel's dream about heaven.

Praying

Jesus, you are my King.
Reign in me and my home,
reign in my life for ever.
Amen.

INDEX OF USES

TOPICS

ACTIVITIES

BIBLE REFERENCES